PAINT IT

The Art of Acrylics, Oils, Pastels, and Watercolors

CAPSTONE PRESS

a capstone imprint

Table of Contents

DREAM IN COLOR.................. 5

WATERCOLORS

IN YOUR ART BOX 8

Watercolor Paints 9

Dot Flower Bouquet 12

Mixed Media................................ 14

Experimental Cupcakes 18

Straw Draw 20

Stylish Mr. Fox 22

Chinese Brush Painting...............24

Shapely Stars 26

Limited Palette............................28

Undersea Wash 30

Cityscape 34

Gouache......................................37

Fashion is Passion.......................38

ACRYLICS

IN YOUR ART BOX 42

Painting With Texture....................46

Dark to Light Abstract...................48

Color Test....................................50

Match the Shade 52

Color-Field..................................54

Blackout......................................56

Eye on Perspective 58

Mayan Art 61

Fantasy Art..................................64

Painting Wildlife...........................66

Four Seasons 70

The Scream in the Dark..................73

PASTELS

IN YOUR ART BOX 78

Rub It In 82

In The Lines................................84

Sharp Points 86

Triple Rainbows 88

Perspectives 90

Scratch-Off.................................92

Batik Heat 94

Soft Edges.................................98

Color Matching 100

Pop Warhol 102

Street Sense..............................104

Over the Top..............................108

OIL PAINTS

IN YOUR ART BOX 112

Transparent and Opaque 116

Tiny Art...................................... 118

Impasto Owl 121

Indirect Sushi 124

Direct Sushi............................... 126

Seurat Dots 128

Picasso's Pets............................ 130

Plein Air 133

In the Style Of 136

Marina Mosaic 141

DREAM IN COLOR

Painting is the way we tell stories and share messages. A single drop of paint can inspire huge murals of color or a series of small, scattered dabs across a canvas.

Pick up a paintbrush or pastel stick, and let your imagination flow through your fingers. Prep your palette, open your mind, and start painting!

IN YOUR ART BOX

Along with crayons and markers, watercolors are some of the first art mediums young artists choose. Watercolors are easy and inviting to use. They can convey the artist's feelings with the flick of a brush. Express your thoughts with just a drop or two of water.

Paints and Pigments

All paints are made up of a pigment and a binder. Pigments are dry, colored powders. They can be natural or artificial. They can come from plants, animals, the earth, or a lab. Pigment is what colors all painting mediums. The only difference between paint mediums is the binder that is used.

Binders are adhesive liquids that hold pigment. Pigment reacts differently depending on the binder that is used. This is why one color of oil paint looks different than the same color of watercolor paint.

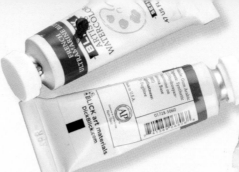

WATERCOLOR PAINTS

From the earliest times, artists painted with watercolors. Primitive artists mixed natural pigments with water or binders like animal fat to decorate personal items or draw the things around them. Today artists use vivid blends of color to paint the world in watercolor.

Watercolors are made with pigments mixed with a binder called gum Arabic. Gum Arabic can be thinned with water. Because of this, watercolors dry quickly and are easy to clean up.

Watercolors are sold in pans or in tubes. Pan watercolors are sold as dry cakes. Tubes hold thick, pastelike paint. Both pan and tube watercolors need to be thinned with water before use. The projects in this book were created with both pan and tube watercolors.

The best kinds of watercolor paints are professional grades. Student grade watercolors are more affordable. However, the quality and consistency are not as reliable.

Some pigments, such as cadmium and cobalt, are toxic. Be careful when working with these pigments. Keep paint away from the mouth and eyes, avoid skin contact whenever possible, and make sure your work space is well ventilated.

PAPERS

Watercolor paper is the most common painting surface. This special paper is designed to absorb water evenly and slowly. It comes in different textures, from smooth, fine-textured paper to bumpy handmade pieces. It should be made of 100 percent cotton or linen. Fine- or medium-textured paper is best for beginners.

Watercolor paper also comes in a variety of weights, from 72 pounds to 300 pounds (150 to 638 grams per square meter.) Thinner paper is less expensive, but also more likely to wrinkle. Many artists stretch their watercolor paper if they are using thinner weights, to prevent wrinkling.

Other commonly used surfaces for watercolors include rice paper, pre-stretched panels, parchment paper, and thin fabrics.

COLOR PALETTE

Watercolor paints come in many premixed colors. However, most artists start with a base palette of between eight and 12 main colors. Below is a list containing some of the more common colors:

French Ultra Blue, Permanent Purple, Cadmium Yellow, Veridiun, Winsor Blue, Winsor Green, Yellow Ochre, Paynes Gray, Brown Madder Alizarin, French Ultramarine, Cadmium Red, Lamp Black, Burnt Sienna, Prussian Blue, Raw Sienna, Indian Red, Alizarin Crimson

Do not store brushes upright. Water can seep into the bristles, causing them to spread. Water will also damage the handles.

BRUSHES

There are many brushes you can use for watercolor painting. They come in a variety of shapes and materials. Natural fibers are the best. The very best brushes are made of 100 percent Russian kolinsky sable hair. Buy the best brushes you can afford, even if you're just starting out. Natural brushes can be expensive. However, a set of quality brushes can last for many years if cared for properly.

Brushes should be cleaned after every painting session. Always handle brushes gently, and always lay them flat.

Different bristles serve different purposes. Flat brushes can make wide strokes or fine edges. Round-tip brushes can be used for almost everything, from bold washes to light detail. Wide or narrow brushes can paint thick or thin lines. Try a variety of brushes to find out which you like best.

Some powerful pigments may stain your brushes. This is OK—just make sure to get all the binder off your brush.

Washing Brushes

Rinse brushes well in lukewarm water. Use a mild soap to lather the brush. Then swirl the bristles on your palm. Rinse, and repeat lathering until no color remains. Wipe gently with a clean rag and let the brushes dry. Store your brushes in a covered drawer or box to keep them clean. Keep brushes with mothballs to prevent moths and other insects from eating your brush bristles.

Round   Flat   Liner   Fan

Dot Flower Bouquet

Get friendly with watercolor! Test the waters by practicing wet-onto-wet and wet-onto-dry techniques. Then create a bouquet pretty enough to give.

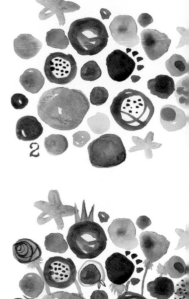

1. Lay paper flat and tape down. Brush paper with water until it no longer absorbs water.

2. Use a round tip brush to apply thinned paint onto paper. Create dots of varied shapes and sizes.

3. While paint is wet, outline flowers with darker shades. Add flower petals using the same technique. Colors should bleed into each other. Layer details to your liking.

4. Add stems. Allow paint to dry.

5. Apply wet watercolors over dried flowers. Experiment with shading and texture. Allow paint to dry.

6. Use a black felt-tip pen to draw leaf details and outline flowers, if desired.

The amount of water you add will affect how much your paint bleeds. Try working with various amounts of paint or water.

Always have at least two containers of water available. One container of clean water should be used for mixing paint. The other should be used to rinse brushes.

Mixed Media

Watercolor paint is fun to experiment with. It reacts differently to many objects. It's easy to move around the page. It shows up on many surfaces, including colored paper and wood. It is easy to thin and can be blotted or smeared. It dries quickly. Once dry, it can be painted over, rubbed, or scratched off. It also works well with other mediums. Search your art box for simple supplies and experiment layering them with watercolors.

Painting Techniques:

~**Wash** A wash is a thin layer of paint spread over a large area. Washes are painted in layers. This creates depth and detail.

~**Glazing** Apply a wash. Allow wash to dry completely. Add another layer. Continue as many times as desired.

~**Graded Wash** Follow instructions for applying a wash. Instead of reloading your brush with paint before every stroke, reload with water. The finished wash will be dark at one end and light at the other.

Glazing

Applying a Wash

Choose a color. Mix the paint, taking care to blend it evenly. Be sure to mix enough for your project.

Begin at the top of the space you want to paint. Tilt the paper slightly. This will encourage the paint to run toward the bottom of the page.

Apply the wash with a wide stroke, working left to right. The color should run to the bottom of the stroke, creating a bead of liquid. Recharge the brush, and apply the next stroke. Be sure that the top of the new stroke touches the bottom of the old stroke. The bead should run to the bottom of your new stroke. Continue applying the wash, working the bead down the painted area.

flat wash   *graded wash*

~**Wet-onto-Wet** Use layers of wet paint to experiment with color mixing and color intensity.

~**Dry Brush** Use a moist paintbrush, but do not thin the paint with water.

~**Scumbling** Lightly paint one color over another, using a fairly dry brush. The underlayer should still be visible.

~**Detail Painting** Use a thin liner brush to add details such as outlines or edges.

~**Push Out Pigment** Lay a wet, used brush over wet paper. Allow the wet paper to pull the color out of the paintbrush.

~**Watercolor Pencils** Use watercolor pencils over wet or dry paint.

Wet-onto-Wet

DRY BRUSH

Scumbling

Detail Painting

Wood

Negative Painting

glue

Watercolor Pencils   *Push out Pigment*

crayon

Black Paper

Paint Over:

~**Glue** Create a pattern with white glue. Allow the glue to dry. Then paint over the dried glue. Your pattern will show through the paint. This is called resist painting.

~**White or Colored Crayon** Use crayon in place of glue for another kind of resist painting.

~**Wood** Use unfinished wood instead of paper.

~**Black or Colored Paper** Use black or colored paper instead of regular watercolor paper.

~**Negative Painting** Paint over waterproof objects such as leaves, tape, or stencils. Once paint is dry, lift or remove the object.

Place On Wet Paint:

~**Wet Thread** Lay wet pieces of string or thread onto wet paint. Remove once paint is dry.

~**Dry Thread** Lay dry pieces of string or thread onto wet paint. Remove once paint is dry.

~**Salt or Sand** Sprinkle onto wet paint. Blow or brush off once paint is dry.

~**Fabric** Lay or press pieces of fabric onto wet paint. Remove once paint is dry.

~**Wet Paint** Drop paint onto wet paper or wet paint.

~**Burlap** Press burlap onto wet paint. The burlap will soak up paint and water, leaving a pattern behind.

DROP COLOR ON WET COLOR

Mix paint by swirling the brush through the paint. Mixing with the tip of your paintbrush is hard on the brush's bristles.

Burlap

Bubble Wrap

Lace

Paint Onto:

~**Burlap** Paint burlap with watery paint. Press burlap onto paper to leave a design.

~**Stamps** Paint stamps and press onto paper.

~**Bubble Wrap** Paint bubble wrap and press onto paper.

~**Lace** Soak lace in watercolors and press firmly onto paper. Use more than one piece to create layers.

~**Sponge** Dab sponge in watercolors. Then dab onto paper.

~**Bread** Soak up paint with bread. Then blot or dab onto paper.

Dab or Rub Wet Paint With:

~**Fabric** Dab or wet paint with pieces of fabric. A rag or an old T-shirt will soak up extra liquid. The pigment will be left behind.

~**Feathers** Use a feather in place of a paintbrush.

Rub Dry Paint With:

~**Eraser** Rub dry paint with eraser.

~**Sandpaper** Lightly scratch away pigment with sandpaper.

Experimental Cupcakes

Take mixed media a step further and create art good enough to eat! Texture brings depth and detail to your paintings. Test it out and create cupcakes that pop.

Bubble Wrap

Sponge

Leaves, Grass or Herbs

Burlap

Bubble Wrap

Sandpaper

Watercolor Pencils

Hardware or Items found in a junk drawer

Peacock Feather

Stretching Watercolor Paper

Lighter-weight watercolor paper needs to be stretched before you start this project. Otherwise, the paper may warp while it dries.

Dip paper into a pan or bucket of water. Make sure it's wetted evenly. Remove the paper. Use a sponge to absorb excess water.

Place the paper onto your work surface. Pin or tape it down with craft paper tape. Use a sponge to smooth the paper and remove any wrinkles or bubbles. Once the paper is completely dry, it is ready to paint.

For most of these cupcakes, start by laying down a wash. Press your material of choice onto the paint. The material can be removed once the paint has dried.

For other cupcakes, try painting directly onto the material. Then blot or press the material onto already-dried watercolor. Test out different amounts of paint. Try using more than one color at a time.

Brush feathers through wet paint or rub sandpaper over dry. See which technique you prefer.

Painting over an object can create a reverse effect.

This is another great project to experiment with the wet-onto-wet and wet-onto-dry techniques.

Add even more detail to your cupcakes with fine paintbrushes or watercolor pencils. Try re-wetting the paper afterward to soften the new lines.

Straw Draw

Think out of the box by applying watercolor without brushes! Start with a simple graded wash. Then use a straw to drip and blow paint across the page. You'll have a spooky forest in no time!

1 Wet paper thoroughly.

2 Using a fan brush, sweep paint across the bottom of the paper.

3 Wet paintbrush before applying each new stroke. Each stroke should be lighter than the last. Continue until the entire paper is covered. Let dry completely.

4 In a cup, mix water and a small amount of black paint. It should look like darkly colored water.

5 Dip a straw into the cup. Use the straw to drip colored water onto the bottom of the paper.

6 Blow through the straw to push the colored water around the paper. Each drip will create a tree branch.

7 Dip a paintbrush into the colored water. Use it to create a base for your spooky trees.

Stylish Mr. Fox

There are many ways to paint the same object. Pick one object and challenge yourself to paint it in three styles—realistic, stylized, and abstract. Can you do it?

Realistic

1 Outline the fox's eyes with a black liner brush.

2 Use a wash to paint the fox's orange fur.

3 Paint the fox's black legs.

4 Thin the black paint to create a lighter gray tone. Use this gray to paint the fox's chest and facial features.

5 Use a liner brush to add depth to the fox's fur. Add various shades of orange with small strokes. The more strokes you add, the thicker the fur will become.

If your paint looks dull, you're probably not using enough water.

What's the Difference?

Realistic: The Realist movement lated from around 1850 to 1870. Realist paintings try to show the expressiveness of real life. See Honoré Daumier and Gustave Courbet.

Stylized: Stylized art falls somewhere between realistic and abstract. Stylized art shows what the artist sees through his or her eyes. See Art Nouveau (1800–1914) and Post-Impressionism (1880–1915).

Abstract: Abstract art began in the early 1900s. Artists used simple shapes and color palettes. They wanted to paint in a freer, more creative way. See Cubism (1907–1920s), Salvador Dalí, and Jackson Pollock.

Stylized

1 Outline the fox's eyes with a black liner brush. Add three black strokes for the legs.

2 Load the liner brush with orange paint. Use it to outline the fox.

3 Use a round tip brush loaded with darker orange paint. Add color under the fox's eyes and to its snout.

4 Thin the black paint to a light gray. Add the fox's fourth leg. The lighter paint shows that the fox's leg is in the background.

5 Continue adding details with the liner brush.

6 Add spots in shades of orange with a small round tip brush.

Abstract

1 Use a liner brush to paint one large eye and one small eye.

2 Connect the eyes with a line. Paint another line at an angle. This will be the fox's nose.

3 Paint a sweeping line between the fox's eyes. Add an ear at each end of the line. Finish outlining the fox's face.

4 Add a tail.

5 Paint the fox's legs.

6 Add more fur to the fox's face and tail with a liner brush.

7 Add spots with a small round tip brush.

23

Chinese Brush Painting

Brush painting originated in China. It quickly became popular throughout southeast Asia. Brush painters use a special ink made of soot and glue. When thinned with water, the ink is called sumi. Brush paintings are traditionally made on rice paper.

Chinese brush painting, also known as *sumi-e*, is a simple and beautiful way to paint with watercolors. Each stroke is "final"—once painted, it cannot be corrected.

1 Thin brown and blue paint in your watercolor tin. Dip your brush into both colors, and paint the tree branch. Paint as much as you can at once.

2 Use quick, short brush strokes to paint the outline of the bird.

3 Use longer and thicker strokes of orange to paint the bird's belly.

Chinese brushes have bamboo handles. The brush is made of absorbent, natural hairs. Each brush is thick and pointed. The harder the brush is pressed, the thicker the painted line will be.

4 Add orange flowers to the branches with light paint strokes. Use darker shades of orange to add depth and shading.

5 Paint the bird's beak. Add light washes of orange to give your bird more life.

蓝色雀

25

Shapely Stars

3

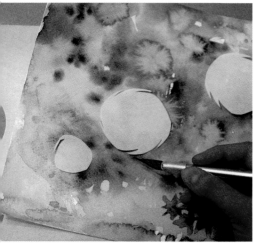

4

5

7

The circles and the plain stars are positive shapes. The stars inside the circles are negative shapes.

Explore the world of positive and negative shapes. Washes, wet-onto-wet techniques, and contact paper will help you create a multilayered piece of art. Use this project to play with colors, shapes, patterns, and brush strokes.

1 Thoroughly wet paper with water.

2 Use a fan brush to sweep green paint over the entire paper.

3 Drop wet purple, yellow, and blue paint randomly onto the paper. Allow the paint droplets to spread naturally. Let dry.

4 Use a craft knife to cut circles out of contact paper. Cut stars out of the circles. Set stars and circles onto the now-dry paper.

5 Place the stars and circles however you like. Then remove backing and stick the shapes onto the paper.

6 Sweep dark blue paint over the entire page. Let dry.

7 Peel contact paper off watercolor paper. Discard.

8 Use white paint to decorate the collage.

Use the heaviest paper possible for this project; 140-pound (300 gsm) or thicker is best.

Limited Palette

Some artists say to paint what you know. Others teach to paint what you see. Why not do both? Get up close and personal with an object that you probably know well—your cell phone.

Limit yourself to a palette of just a few colors. Then get to work personalizing your phone!

1:27

Applying thinned transparent paint over a dry wash is called glazing. Using multiple glazes makes rounded objects pop. Use the side of your brush to add shadows to your cell phone's screen.

Transparent paint lets the white of the watercolor paper show through. Opaque paint blocks the white. To see whether paint is transparent or opaque, apply it over a line of black paint. The paint is transparent if the black shows through. If it shows over the black paint, the paint is opaque.

1 Draw two rectangles with rounded corners.

2 Saturate your brush with water. Use pink to paint the hibiscus flowers onto the case and the phone screen.

3 Blend peach paint into the pink to give the flowers more depth. Let dry.

4 Paint thin, black lines inside the flowers. Add speaker and button details to the cell phone.

5 Dot the flowers with pink and peach paint.

6 Paint the cell phone screen blue. Using a contrasting color will help the flower stand out.

Undersea Wash

Adding drawings to a watercolor painting is a great idea. But the pressure of perfection scares many new artists. Tracing paper removes the risk of ruining your already awesome artwork. Sketch yourself some smiling fish. Then trace them once they're just the way you want them!

Rubbed Off

Watercolor paper has a special layer of gum that helps it absorb paint. If you erase on watercolor paper, you also erase some of that layer.

To skip the rubbing step, use graphite transfer paper. This paper is already coated with graphite. Just place the image over the graphite paper and trace.

1 Brush paper with wet brush until the paper no longer absorbs water.

2 Use a fan brush to apply a wash of blue paint. Let dry.

3 Draw fish onto tracing paper using a graphite pencil.

4 Turn tracing paper over. Using the side of your pencil, rub graphite all over the back of your drawing. Rub the graphite with a tissue or cotton ball. Blow or shake off any extra graphite dust.

continued on next page

5 Cut out each fish.

6 Turn the tracing paper back over so the rubbed graphite is on the bottom. Place fish onto the painted paper. Arrange them however you like.

7 Using your pencil, re-trace your fish. This will transfer the fish onto the painted paper. Trace hard enough to transfer your lines without scratching your watercolor paper.

Avoid using dull pencils when tracing your fish. Sharp (or mechanical) pencils will make clear, easy-to-see lines.

Reshaping your Brushes

If your brushes look too ragged for this project, try reshaping them.

First, wash your brush in hot, soapy water until the bristles soften. Then gently shape the bristles the way you want. Dip the softened bristles into a gentle shampoo or hair gel. Then allow the brush to air dry.

After the brush is dry, rinse gently until no soap remains.

Smudge-Free

Carefully lift your fish off the watercolor paper after tracing. Wash your hands, and blow any graphite dust off the paper. Loose dust will cause smudging.

For extra smudge protection, dip the tissue or cotton ball in rubbing alcohol. Then use it to smooth the graphite backing in step 4.

Keep your drawings simple. Too many lines can smudge once you start painting. This can make your watercolors appear muddy.

8 Use a round-tip brush to paint the fish. Test out contrasting colors and multiple washes. This will help bring your fish to life.

9 Add details, such as scales and gills, to the fish with a liner brush.

10 Add waves and bubbles to the water.

9

Cityscape

It's easy to paint your favorite photo with watercolors. But why make an exact copy? Instead, focus on the space's lights and darks (values), shades (tones), and basic shapes.

1. Create the background wash. Use a fan brush and green and blue paints.

2. Add the basic shapes of the trees in the foreground.

3. Add a variety of color tones to represent the trees in the background. Don't be concerned with shape or size. Just focus on the light and dark areas.

4. Add more layers of color to the grass and sky.

5. Using a flat brush, add rectangles of color. These will represent the buildings. Focus on the shapes of the buildings, not the buildings themselves.

6. Continue adding layers of color. Focus on the shadowed sides of the buildings.

Show-off

Thin mat boards both protect and show off your art. Mat boards have a black piece and a front piece. The front piece has a window cut out of it to frame your artwork.

Watercolors for show are usually matted and framed. Clear sheets of glass or plastic, called glazing, protect your art from dirt and natural light. For extra protection, a varnish made of beeswax can be added.

For best results, hang paintings in a temperature-controlled area. Keep them out of direct sunlight.

7. Use a liner brush to add shape to the background trees.

8. Add leaves and branches to the trees in the foreground.

Gouache

"Gouache" (GWASH) means "water paint" in Italian. Gouache is a type of opaque watercolor. Gouache is great because it dries quickly. The vivid colors make it great for layering. Try applying it dark-to-light to make an eye-catching piece of art. Grab a tube of this opaque watercolor and make a splash!

1 Create a quick sketch of the cityscape and the hot air balloons.

2 Once you are happy with your sketch, paint it onto a piece of thicker watercolor paper. Focus on the darker areas of the drawing while noting details such as light sources and rounded areas. Let the underpainting dry completely before continuing.

3 Add color to your painting, working dark to light.

4 Finish your painting by adding details with a fine liner brush.

Don't worry if your gouache dries out on your palette. Dried gouache can be rewetted and reused.

Use a heavier paper when working with gouache. The paint's thicker texture can cause lighter paper to warp.

37

Fashion is Passion

Work in layers with this cool collage project! Collage is a technique that layers paper and other material onto paintings. It adds texture and depth to any piece of artwork. Combine collage with watercolor and explore art that pops off the page.

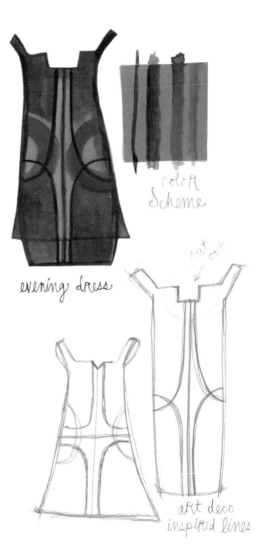

color scheme

evening dress

cut out

art deco inspired lines

Collage has been used throughout history and around the world. Pablo Picasso (1881–1973) is often credited as being the first to use collage in fine art. See also Henry Matisse (1869–1955) and the Futurist movement.

1. Sketch the item of clothing you want onto heavyweight paper.

2. Choose a piece of patterned or textured rice paper. This is what you'll use to create your collage. Stain rice paper with watercolor paint. Let dry completely.

3. Cut out the clothing item sketched in Step 1 from the now-dry paper. Place the cutout over the sketch, and glue onto the heavyweight paper.

4. Use a watercolor pencil to add details such as pockets or seams.

5. Continue collaging layers and details of the outfit using paper in other colors, patterns, and textures.

Summer Dress

Skirt

Wrap Dress

Tissue paper or masa paper are other lightweight papers that work well for collage. For a different look, try using stamps, bits of magazine or newspaper, wrapping paper, tickets, or wallpaper.

acrylics

IN YOUR ART BOX

Acrylic paint knows no limits! You can use it to paint a masterpiece or create crafts. Put paintbrush to paint and decorate in the world in acrylics.

ACRYLIC PAINTS

When compared to other painting mediums, acrylics are new to the art world. They first appeared in the 1940s.

Although acrylic paints resemble oils, there are things that set them apart. Acrylic paints use a binder called acrylic resin. This resin dries quickly and is still flexible. Used alone, acrylic resin can be used as a glue.

Acrylic paints can be thinned with mineral spirits or water.

Pigments used for oil paintings can be used for acrylic paints too. The amount of pigment used can change the way the paint looks. Less pigment can give your paints the look of watercolors. Add more and they will look like oils.

Use acrylic paint anywhere!
Paper, cardstock, wood, or canvas are common surfaces.

You can buy paper specifically designed for acrylic paints.
These sheets of paper resemble actual canvas. You can also
buy panels mounted with pieces of canvas. The canvas will be
pre-primed, which will help your paintings last longer.

BRUSHES AND KNIVES

A variety of brushes means a variety of textures and strokes in your art. Buy the best brushes you can afford, even if you're just starting out. A good basic set includes three round brushes of various sizes, a detail round brush, and a full-belly round brush.

Brushes used for acrylic painting need to be soaked during use. This keeps the paints in the brush bristles from drying out. Natural-bristle brushes can lose their shape if soaked often. Synthetic brushes might be a better choice if you plan on doing a lot of acrylic painting.

Dried acrylic paint is very difficult to remove from brush bristles. Soaking in strong solvents might remove the paint. However, the solvents can also damage the brush.

Go beyond brushes and try out a painting knife. Painting knives are used to apply paint. Palette knives are used for cleaning your palette. Spatulas and scrapers can be used to mix paint. You can also use them to scrape paint onto your painting. Start with a basic, quality painting knife made of tempered steel. If you like what it does, you can always buy more.

Palette knives come in a variety of shapes and sizes.

TIPS AND TECHNIQUES

Practice your brush strokes to find the techniques that work best for you. Try:

~**Tape Masking** Use tape to create designs on paper. Paint over the tape. Remove once paint is dry. Create multiple layers, if desired.

~**Hard and Soft Edges** Practice blocking in color to create hard and soft edges. Experiment with old credit cards, stencils, stamps, and palette knives for hard edges. Rags, thick bristle brushes, and water are good for soft edges.

~**Scumbling** Apply paint in a crosshatch pattern to experiment with scumbling.

~**Wet Paint** Try thinning the paint with water. Apply your watery paint in drips or splashes.

Tape Masking

Hard edge & Soft edge

Crosshatch Brush Stroke

Stay Safe!

The Art and Creative Materials Institute (ACMI) tests art supplies. They make sure paints are properly labeled.

Supplies with the AP seal from ACMI are certified nontoxic. Nontoxic items will not cause major health problems in people.

Supplies with the CL label do potentially contain toxic or hazardous materials. However, with appropriate handling they can be used safely. Directions on the container or package should be followed exactly.

ACMI
AP
ART & CREATIVE MATERIALS INSTITUTE CERTIFIED
Conforms to ASTM D 4236

ACMI
CL
ART & CREATIVE MATERIALS INSTITUTE CERTIFIED
Conforms to ASTM D 4236

~**Sgraffito** Scrape off wet or dry paint with a palette knife or other sharp item.

~**Dry Brush** Practice various brush strokes with a dry brush to see how they look in layers.

~**Stencils and Stamps** Use stencils and stamps to create texture and patterns. Your fingers are the perfect natural stamp!

~**Wet And Dry** Apply wet paint to wet paper. Also try using a very wet brush on dry paper.

Sgraffito Technique

Dry Brush

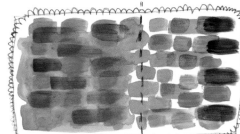

Wet Brush on Wet Paper   *Wet Brush on Dry Paper*

Acrylic paint dries quickly. Thickly applied areas of paint need only a day or two to dry.

Stencil & Stamp Painting

Apply Paint with a Card

COLOR PALETTE

Acrylic paints come in many premixed colors. However, most artists start with a base palette of between eight and 12 main colors. Below is a list containing some of the more common colors:

Lemon Yellow, Azo Yellow Medium, Cadmium Red Light, Permanent Rose, Permanent Alizarin Crimson, Ultramarine Blue, Phthalo Blue Green Shade, Phthalo Green Blue Shade, Raw Umber, Yellow Ochre, Burnt Sienna, and Titanium White.

Some pigments are toxic. If you're not sure whether a pigment is toxic, check the label. Many toxic pigments have a metal in their name, such as copper, cadmium, cobalt, and lead.

Finger Painting

Painting With Texture

Thick layers of paint create swirling white waves and sandy beaches. This technique, called impasto, gives an almost 3D feel. Create this tropical texture by painting with palette knives and gel medium.

1 Apply paint thickly to the canvas. Use the back of a palette knife to paint the sky and the beach.

2 Try a variety of palette knives to paint the water. Experiment with dabbing, layering, and adding swirls. Alternate between using white and shades of blue.

3 Use the tip of a palette knife to add palm trees. Apply the paint with the flat part. Use the edges and tip to create the leaves on the tree.

4 Mix sand with the paint you use to paint the beach. Add the sandy paint in multiple layers.

Use a thick gel medium to give your waves more texture.

Gel medium is an unpigmented acrylic liquid. It extends the drying time for acrylic paint. It can be used to smooth out or thicken paint. It can also be used like glue.

BASICS
gloss fluid medium
use with acrylic paint
médium liquide brillant
medio fluido brillante
250ml ℮ 8.79 US. fl.oz

Make sure your palette knife is not too sharp. A sharp knife can cut right through your canvas (or your skin!) If your knife is too sharp, it can be dulled by rubbing the edge with sandpaper.

Dark to Light Abstract

Layers of flat paint can have just as much depth as impasto paintings. Start with a plain black canvas. Shed some light with increasingly light circles. Make colors pop with a splash of yellow.

Acrylic paint dries quickly. Squeeze out small amount of paints to minimize waste.

1 Paint a white canvas all black. Let dry.

2 Fill the canvas with dark blue circles.

3 Add a bit of white paint to the blue before painting more circles. Vary the circles' sizes and positions.

4 Continue adding white circles until your top layer is nearly covered.

5 Add yellow circles.

6 Add gold circles.

7 Don't stop now. Add as many layers as you want. Try going backward, adding more dark blue paint to the white.

Try applying paint without brushes. Rags, sponges, or your fingers are great alternatives!

49

Color Test

Experiment with color! Create a grid
and test out different color and shape
combinations. Outline your squares with
black to make them look like stained glass.

*Quilting patterns are
another great inspiration
for geometric shapes.*

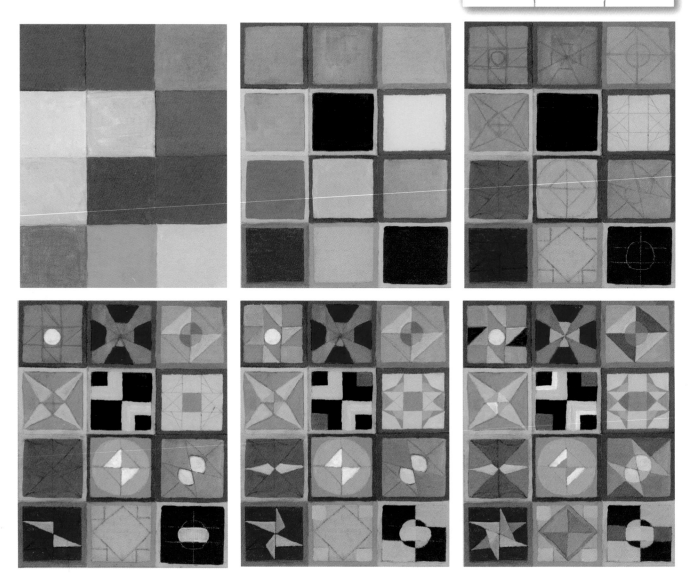

1 Use a ruler to draw even squares on your canvas.

2 Paint each square a different color. Let dry.

3 Use a pencil to lightly sketch geometric shapes into each square.

4 Paint each of the geometric shapes you drew. Let dry.

5 Turn your shapes into stained glass by outlining all the edges with black marker.

Flat-edged brushes work best for putting fine lines on your geometric shapes.

Match the Shade

52

Acrylic paint dries two shades darker. Keep that in mind when mixing wet paint for this project.

You don't need a huge rainbow of color to create vivid paintings. Pick a picture to recreate. Identify the base colors used in that image. Then stick to them.

1 Use painting tape to mask off a square of your canvas paper.

2 Draw light grid lines to help map out the placement of the balloons. Draw the balloons in pencil.

3 Using only the two shades of pink, paint the balloons.

4 Paint the sky using only the two shades of blue.

5 Create the clouds using the light blue paint. Use a small fan brush to soften the clouds' edges.

6 Use a thin liner brush to add the balloon strings.

Color-Field

Color-Fields

Color-fields were first painted in the 1950s. Artists wanted to create pieces that were modern, abstract, and bright. See works by Helen Frankenthaler, Kenneth Nolan, and Morris Louis.

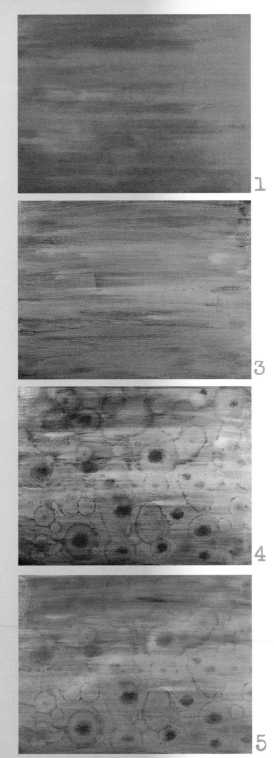

This project uses isopropyl alcohol, which can be found at drugstores. Use at least 91 percent alcohol. Some stores sell 70 percent alcohol, but that isn't strong enough to create the desired layers.

New artists sometimes have a hard time filling the whole canvas. Get over your fears by creating a huge color-field.

1 Paint your canvas any color you want. Be sure to fill the entire space. Let dry.

2 Choose another color. Use a small plastic cup to mix two parts water to one part paint.

3 Use a large, fat-ended brush to coat the entire canvas with the watered-down paint. Do not let dry.

4 Drip alcohol onto the canvas before the paint dries. The alcohol will repel the watery paint and let the base layer of paint show through.

5 Let the alcohol and water paint dry. Continue adding as many layers of watery paint and alcohol as you want.

For more layering, drip watery paint in different colors onto the canvas. Allow paint to run together and blend before adding the alcohol.

Blackout

Did you notice that black wasn't in the Color Palette list at the beginning of the chapter? That's because you can make your own! Black from a tube can overpower your other paints. You can get a more diverse black depending on which colors you mix.

1 Test and compare different color blends, including:
~Prussian Blue/Burnt Sienna
~Raw Umber/Prussian Blue
~Burnt Umber/Ultramarine Blue

Test out and compare different color blends. Each black will be subtly different.

2 Once you've tested each color combination, mix each with a bit with white. This will show the color mixture's undertone.

3 After you're done experimenting, challenge yourself! Pick a picture to paint in black and white—without using true black.

4 Roughly layer different colors to create the wooden fence's texture.

5 Paint the shape of the skates.

6 Add details to the skates, including the laces, stitching, and blades.

Burnt Sienna | Prussian Blue Raw Umber | Prussian Blue Burnt Umber | Ultramarine Blue

Black

Mix your paints on your palette thoroughly.

Eye on Perspective

Animal eyes come in all shapes, sizes, and colors. Stare
them down and study them closely! Focus on light, colors,
and details to make these eyes as real as possible.

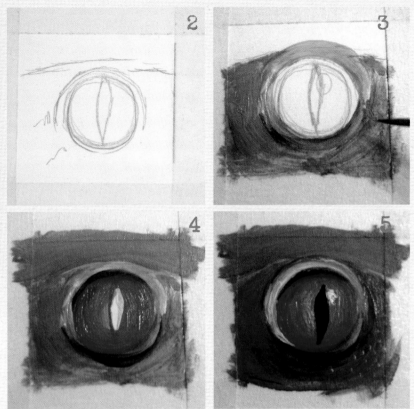

Keep your fine-tip brushes free of excess paint. This will ensure clean lines in your detail work.

1 Use painter's tape to mask off even squares across your canvas.

2 Draw a rough sketch of an eye in each square.

3 Begin by painting the area around the eye. Add general color tones. You will go back and paint small details later.

4 Paint the actual eye. Work with the main base color. Then add color and shading to give the eye a rounded shape. Paint dark-to-light, bottom-to-top for the most natural feel.

5 Use small-tipped brushes to add highlights to the area around the eye. Blend paint to add light and shadows.

continued on next page

Find close-up photographs of animal eyes to use for reference. Nature magazines, Internet searches, and other database-type websites will help you find vivid shots.

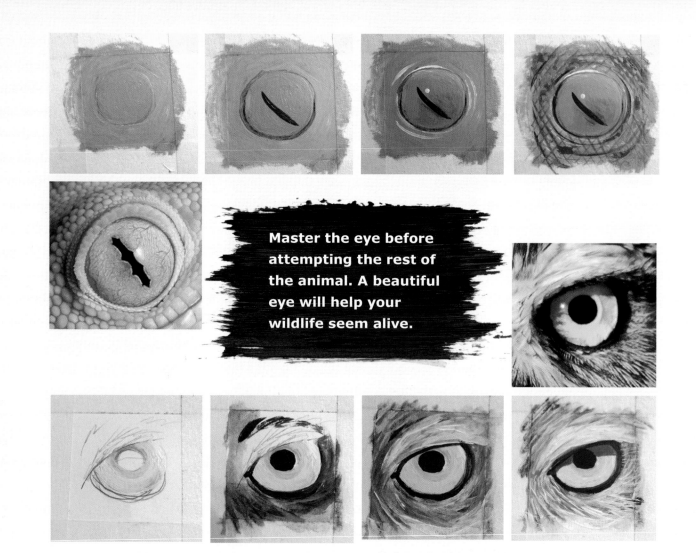

Master the eye before attempting the rest of the animal. A beautiful eye will help your wildlife seem alive.

6 Once paint is dry, carefully peel off tape.

7 Carefully cut out each square. Leave a border around each square, if desired. To skip the cutting step, paint your eyes on artist trading cards.

8 Laminate or varnish each square for extra protection.

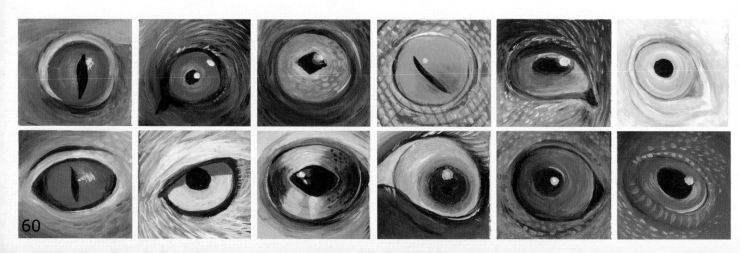

Mayan Art

continued on next page

Use the sgraffito technique to scratch out Mayan-inspired art. Use household items to scratch away layers of paint and expose colorful underlayers.

1 Paint a circle with acrylic paint. Let dry.

2 Mix white paint with an equal amount of gel medium.

3 Paint a bird in the middle of the circle. Do not allow paint to dry.

4 Quickly use a key to scrape long and short lines off the bird's wings and body.

5 Mix black paint with gel medium. Paint the space above the bird. Do not allow paint to dry.

6 Use a nail to draw lines into the black paint. Scratch hard enough to allow color underneath to show through.

7 Add details to the bird, such as beak and chest feathers.

8 Mix red paint with gel medium. Paint the space below the bird. Do not allow paint to dry.

9 Use a pencil eraser to scratch the star and moon into the red paint.

10 Draw zigzags around the circle with red and yellow paint. Let dry.

11 Mix light gray with gel medium. Paint a large circle over and around the yellow and red zigzags.

12 Use an old toothbrush to push the gray paint out, toward the edges of the circle.

13 Use the pencil eraser to scratch over the zigzag pattern. This will expose the red paint underneath.

14 Paint around the zigzag with black paint.

15 Mix red and yellow paint with gel medium. Paint around the whole image one last time. Do not let dry.

16 Use a hair comb to scratch waves around the outer layer.

Some gel mediums come premixed with glass, pumice, or small pieces of acrylic. These give the gel different properties, such as a shiny surface or a rough texture. Try using one or all of these gels for added effect.

Fantasy Art

Have you ever looked out your window and wished your view was of something different? Grab a paintbrush, buy a window to paint, and make it happen! Bring your dream view to life with this fantasy art project.

If you can't find a window, use a sheet of clear acrylic. Both windows and acrylic sheets can be found at home improvement stores.

1 Wash the window thoroughly. Make sure all traces of window cleaner have been removed.

2 If you're worried about painting onto the wood, mask the edges of the window with painter's tape.

3 Think about what you want to paint. Planning ahead is important for this project. Mistakes can be corrected, but fixes can take time.

4 Dip a round-tipped brush into pink paint. Then dip it into red paint. Then dip it into orange paint. This will create a layered effect as you paint the flowers.

5 Swirl the paint onto the glass. The layered paint will blend together. Add as many flowers as you wish. Let dry.

6 Paint green vines and leaves for the flowers.

Varnish

Most acrylic paintings should be varnished. Varnish protects your paintings from light damage, humidity, and dust. It is sold in spray cans and as a liquid to brush on.

Apply varnish outdoors or in a well-ventilated room. Allow your paint to dry between 48 and 72 hours before adding varnish.

If using brush-on varnish, apply in one to three thin, even coats. Overlap each brush stroke slightly. Do not go back over wet varnish. This can cause a cloudy appearance. Allow at least 12 hours before applying another coat.

7 Add a fence to the background. Let dry completely.

8 Paint the birds and any remaining flower details.

9 To protect your art, you'll need to seal the paint. This is especially important because paint can be scratched or washed off glass. Acrylic varnish works best. Follow the safety tips in the sidebar above.

To fix a mistake, press a paper towel dipped in window cleaner onto the paint. Then use a razor blade to gently scrape paint off the glass.

Painting Wildlife

Zoom out and take your eye study and color matching skills to the next level. Pick a photo, trace your tiger, and get painting!

make eyes farther apart!

show more chin!

Why Thumbnails?

Thumbnails help you plan ahead. You can decide what part of the painting will be the central focus before you begin. Thumbnails will also help you see the light and dark shades, called values. This will help save you time and materials once you begin painting.

1 Paint a masonite board with cream-colored paint. Let dry.

2 Select a photo. Use it to create at least two thumbnail sketches. The two thumbnails should have different focal points and values.

3 Draw the picture of the tiger onto tracing paper. Try to capture the values chosen in the thumbnail.

continued on next page

5

4 Turn the tracing paper over. Rub the back of the paper with an even layer of graphite.

5 Flip the paper back over. Place the tiger image over the masonite board. Use a pencil to trace over your drawing and transfer it onto the board.

6 Use a fan brush to create the tiger's white fur.

7 Add the tiger's black stripes.

8 Start with burnt orange paint. Blend until you have a shade of orange that matches your tiger.

9 Begin painting the tiger's orange parts. Start with the larger spaces first and work your way into the more detailed areas.

Start with the white areas first. This will help the orange blend naturally.

6

7

8

9

10 Continue layering orange paint of various shades and tones until tiger is completely painted.

11 Paint the tiger's eyes and nose. Start with the dark pupil. Add color in layers to give the eye a more lifelike feel.

12 Use a liner brush to paint the tiger's whiskers.

Go back and touch your tiger up where necessary. Add light strokes of white paint to mimic layers of fur.

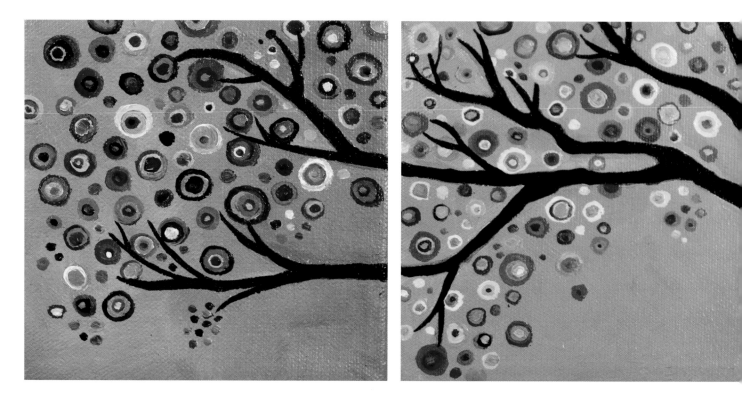

Four Seasons

Build from the ground up with this color-field that spans all four seasons. Use skills already mastered, such as color-fields, abstract circles, and color matching, and take this project to the next level of difficulty.

1 Use thumbnails and miniature paintings to plan your painting. Decide color palettes and patterns before starting on full-sized panels.

2 Lightly sketch a tree that spans across all four panels.

3 Paint the rough shape of the tree.

4 Paint the background color for each canvas. Let dry.

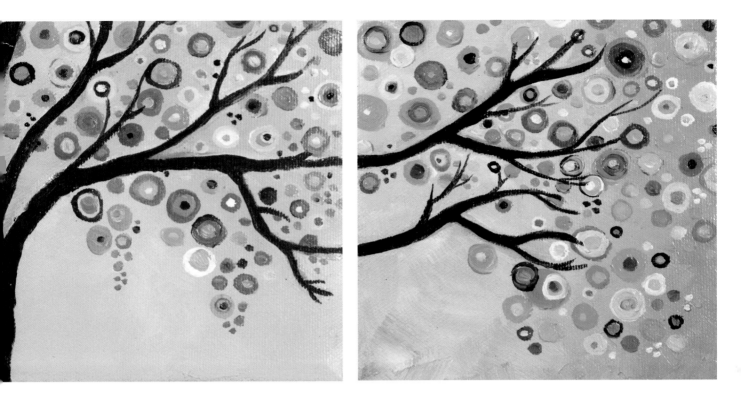

continued on next page

71

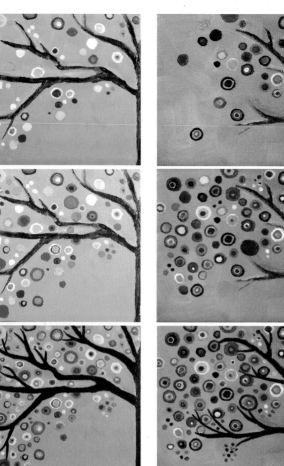

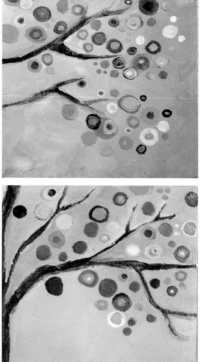

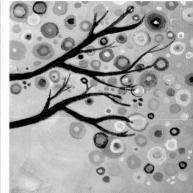

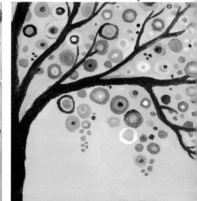

For extra flair, paint the background colors first. Use rubbing alcohol to create color-fields before adding the tree branches.

5 Starting with one panel, paint small dots around the tree. Round-tipped brushes work well for this.

6 Continue layering dots and circles in varying colors around the branches.

7 Add more branches to the tree to make it look more full.

8 Finish detailing the tree with dark brown paint to add bark texture.

The Scream in the Dark

continued on next page

A man screams on the edge of a bridge. The water and sky behind him is wavy and distorted. This painting, called *The Scream*, is recognizable all over the world. Take out your paintbrush, grab some glow-in-the-dark paints, a black light, and flip off the lights. Can you make your canvas scream too?

Choose a bright white surface to paint on. The whiter the paper, the greater your paints will glow.

1 Paint the sky, water, and rough shape of the bridge. Keep your strokes bold and abstract.

2 Add the scream character, starting with basic white and black.

3 Build the bridge railing. Start with the darkest colors and working toward the lightest.

4 Use yellow to add highlights to the sky, water, and bridge.

5 Add final touches to the water, the scream character, and the bridge railing.

6 Because flourescent paint is not lightfast, varnish with UltraViolet Light Stabilizers (UVLS) if desired.

Use blacklight-sensitive neon paint for this project. The paint can be mixed, but will glow the brightest if used straight from the bottle.

74

The Scream

When Norwegian artist Edvard Munch (1863–1944) died, thousands of pieces of art were found in his home. But *The Scream* is the one most people remember.

Munch made four versions of this painting—two with paint and two with pastels. In 2012 Munch's pastel and cardboard version sold for nearly $120 million. It set a world record for any work of art sold at auction.

See Expressionism (1905–1925), Vincent van Gogh, and Paul Gauguin.

For an extra challenge, use invisible UV paint. This paint brushes on clear, but glows brightly under UV light.

IN YOUR ART BOX

Pastels don't come in a tube and aren't applied with a brush. But these smudgeable, smearable, grown-up crayons use pigment. Because of this, pastels are considered paint. In fact, they were the very first paints used by people. Give these sticks of pigment a try and make them first in your art book.

PASTELS

Many people find pastels to be the easiest paint medium to work with. Pastels don't need time to dry, and no special tools are required. They don't crack, darken, or change color over time. They can be applied in any order, so there's no need to paint light to dark. And they can be used on almost any kind of paper.

Although pastels are the most basic paint medium, they come in many varieties. The color wheel above shows soft pastels (outer circle), oil pastels (middle circle), and pastel pencils (inner circle).

Soft Pastels: Soft pastels are sold as thick sticks. They are made of pigment mixed with binder and white coloring. Soft pastels contain the smallest amount of binder. They draw soft, easy-to-smudge lines.

Hard Pastels: Hard pastels are sold as thin sticks. They are made with more binder. This means that colors may fade. They can be sharpened and draw thin, even lines.

Pastel Pencils: Pastel pencils are like regular pencils, but with cores of pastel instead of lead. They can also be sharpened. Pastel pencils are good for narrow lines and detail work. Like hard pastels, they can fade over time.

Oil Pastels: Oil pastels are sold as thick sticks wrapped in paper. They are sometimes called wax crayons. Oil pastels are made of pigment mixed with an oil or wax binder. They make a thick, greasy line that can be smudged with turpentine or mineral spirits.

Chalk: Chalk is made by mixing natural minerals with an oil binder. Artist's chalk is different from the chalk used on chalkboard, which contains no binder.

TIPS AND TECHNIQUES

Pastels are easy to use and easy to experiment with.
Grab a few sticks, start sketching, and get creative!

~Draw with the tip of the pastel stick. Use the side of the stick to paint.

~Use a sharp knife to sharpen pastels. Sandpaper is a good tool to shape the pastels into points.

~Tap loose powder off your paper as you work. This will help keep your workspace clean. It will also help additional layers of color cling to the paper.

~Limit direct skin contact with hazardous pigments, especially if you use professional grade pastels. Try to use paper, blending sticks, or cloth to blend instead of your finger whenever possible. This prevents toxic materials from entering through your skin.

Thumbnails are a great way to experiment with pastels. Miniatures that you really like can be blown up to full-sized projects later.

~To clean pastels, wipe each stick with a paper towel. To give a thorough cleaning, place a handful of cornmeal in a container with a lid. Add a few pastels at a time. Shake gently for a minute or two or until pastels are completely clean.

Many simple techniques can be used with pastels. Practice blending and layering until you feel comfortable working with each kind of pastel.

~Pastels can smear easily. Spray finished pieces with fixative or frame them under glass. Follow all safety instructions while using fixative.

~When using pastels, work in a well-ventilated area. Gloves and a mask give extra protection from pastel dust. Be sure to wash up well afterward!

COLOR PALETTE

Pastels can be purchased in individual sticks or in sets of six, 12, 24, or more. Before buying the biggest set, think about how much you plan on using them. Think about storage too. Pastels must be kept clean and organized. If you plan on traveling with your pastels, consider weight. Pastels are heavy. The more you buy, the more you'll have to carry with you.

Try to buy pastels with natural pigments, such as ochres, umbers, and oxides. They are less likely to fade over time.

Rub It In

Get started with simple experimenting. Grab some everyday blending tools and a cup of water. Then find out what you can do with a simple box of pastels.

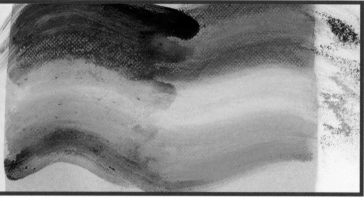

Wet and Dry

Your first rainbow will explore how soft pastels blend using brushes. How do they behave when dry? How do they behave when wet?

1 Draw a rainbow across your paper. Blend half the rainbow with a wet paintbrush.

2 Blend the other half of the rainbow with a dry paintbrush.

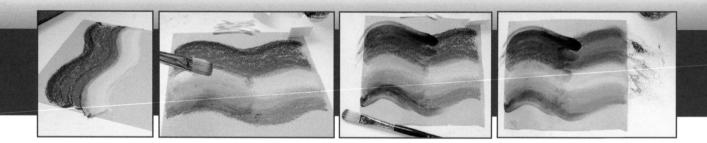

Soft Swabs

The object you use for blending can change the way your pastels look.

1 Blend the rainbow lines with a dry cotton swab.

2 Reblend the rainbow lines with a wet cotton swab. The wet lines will dry lighter than the others.

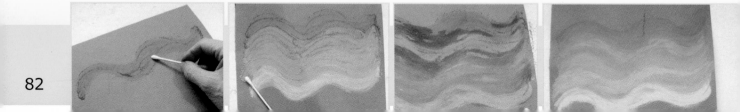

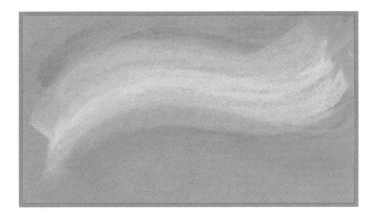

Blended 'bow

A makeup sponge can soften pastels. The colors flow together and become light and airy. Compare this rainbow to the one blended with the cotton swab.

1 Draw dark, rich lines onto your pastel paper.

2 Blend the colors with a makeup sponge. Notice how the sponge softens the lines.

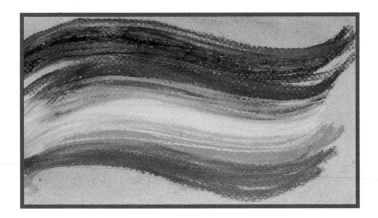

Painted Pastels

This rainbow shows another way water affects pastels.

1 Wet your pastel paper. For an even coat of water, use a thick, soft paintbrush.

2 Draw over the wet paper with pastels. Notice how the lines hold their shape.

In The Lines

Play with pastels to paint this colorful prism. Each color stripe shows a different technique to use with oil pastels.

1 Mask the edges of the paper and tape to your work station.

2 Lightly sketch the prism onto the paper.

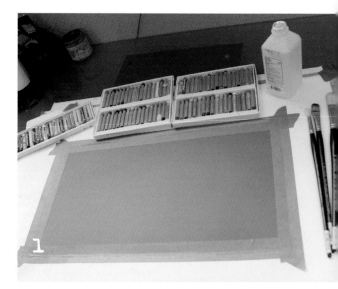

The kind of paper used can change how the final painting looks. Colored paper may show through the pigment. It can also help the pastel colors pop. Textured paper gives the pastels something to grab onto. The more textured the paper, the deeper the pigments appear.

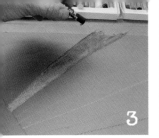

3 Begin with the purple stripe. Color the stripe using fine parallel lines. Then add a second layer of lines going a slightly different direction to create cross-hatching.

4 Color the next line blue. Use a paintbrush to smear the line with rubbing alcohol.

5 Color the next stripe light green. Then set a cold cookie sheet over the paper (or put the paper in the freezer.)

While the paper is chilling, warm the end of a dark green pastel by holding it against a heating pad or coffee cup warmer. Use the hot pastel stick to color over the light green stripe on the cold paper. The pastel should create a thick, saturated dark green stripe over the light green.

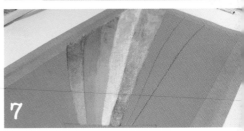

6 Color the next stripe light yellow. Blend part of a dark yellow pastel stick with linseed oil. Paint over the light yellow with the thinned dark yellow.

7 Brush the next stripe with linseed oil. Then color directly over the oil with an orange pastel stick.

8 Use glue to design a pattern over the next stripe. Let dry completely. Color over the dried glue with a red-orange pastel stick.

9 Color the red stripe by moving your pastel stick in tight circles.

Sharp Points

Give your art a fine point with pastel pencils. Most artists find pastel pencils easy to hold and less messy than regular pastels. Compare the many ways pastel pencils can be used by lining them up as a crafty chevron.

1 Use a ruler, pencil, and scissors to measure and cut out rectangles from white and colored paper.

2 Decorate each rectangle using a different color or technique.

3 Once you're done experimenting, arrange the strips into a rainbow chevron pattern. Glue the pieces together onto a piece of paper.

Glazes and Scumbles

A **glaze** is a transparent layer of dark paint over light opaque paint. Glazes give paintings the appearance of depth.

A **scumble** is a layer of light paint applied over darker paint. Scumbling is one way to add light to paintings.

Try some of these techniques to get familiar with pastel pencils!

~Blend with water, rubbing alcohol, or linseed oil

~Blend with cotton swabs, paintbrushes, or blending sticks

~Use white, colored, or textured paper

~Layer different shades of the same colors together

~Layer different colors

~Gently rub the side of the pastel over a colored base. This will blend and soften the layers, creating a glaze or scumble.

~Paint using cross-hatching. Have the first layer of lines be one color. Paint the top layer another color.

~Paint thin lines of one color. Then paint thin lines of another color going the same way on top of the first lines. This will create a feathering effect.

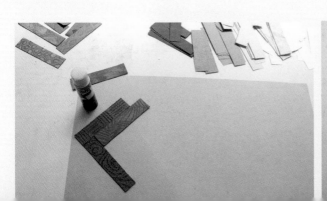

Triple Rainbows

Black paper is the perfect tool to let pastels shine. Use what you learned about the different pastel types to create a larger-than-life masterpiece.

Sanded black pastel paper will hold the most pigment. The textured surface gives pigment something to grab onto.

2

1 Begin by drawing some large, flowing lines across the paper. Try to use the entire paper.

2 Continue adding to the flowing lines. Use a variety of pastel types. (The blue dots are oils, the orange and green lines are medium, and the red lines are pencil.)

3 Create layers with oil pastels.

4 Build color by creating soft pastel rainbows. Then blend them together.

5 Blend regular pastels around and into the oil circles.

6 Use pastel pencils to create sharp lines between contrasting colors.

7 Don't be afraid to change the direction and flow of the lines. Let the lines come naturally.

Make a mistake? Grab an old toothbrush. Lightly brush over whatever you want to erase.

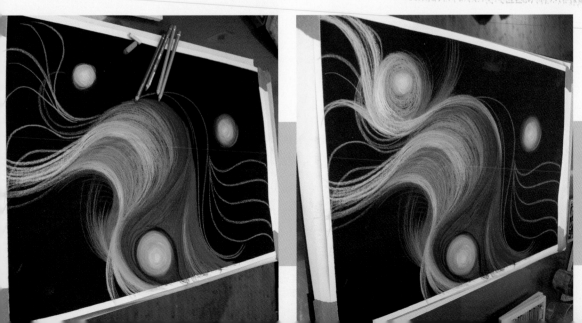

Let some of the black paper show through. This will create natural shading and dimension.

Perspectives

Create interest in your art by drawing a bright focal
point. A painting's focal point pulls the viewer's eye
right to it. Take a lesson in perspective. Soon you'll
have a piece of art that people can't stop staring at.

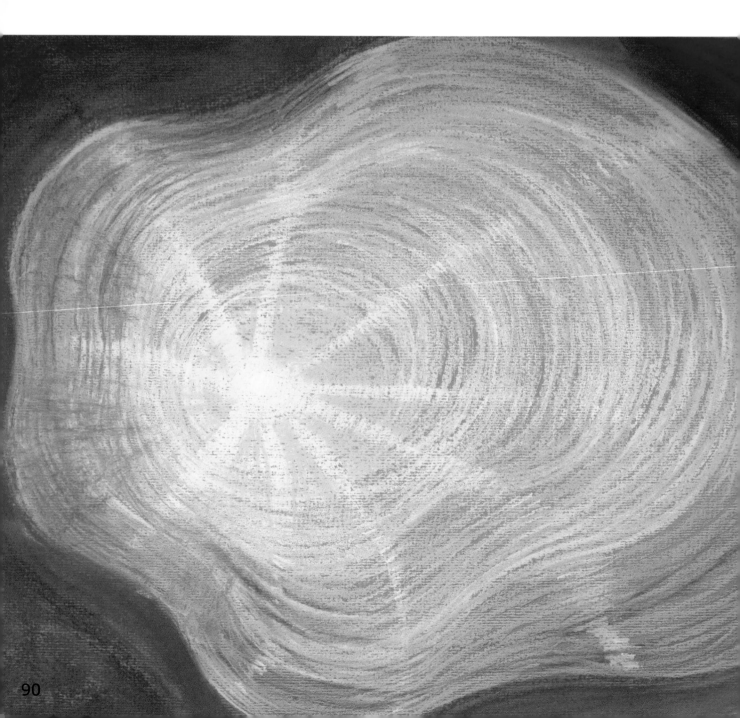

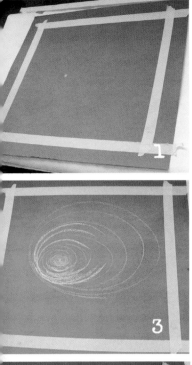

1. Use tape to mask off a square on your paper.

2. Choose the focal point for your masterpiece. Mark it with a light dot.

3. Begin sketching circles around your focal point to create a tunnel.

4. Give the tunnel outer edges. The edges should be a different color.

5. Draw perspective lines coming from the center of the tunnel. The lines will give your tunnel a more 3D feel.

6. Continue adding "walls" to your tunnel.

7. Add highlights to the light at the end of the tunnel.

8. Add highlights and shadows to the tunnel walls.

9. As a final step, darken the outside edges of the tunnel. Remove tape when completely finished.

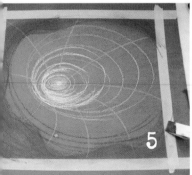

Make sure your colored paper was dyed with permanent pigments. This ensures that the colors won't fade.

Scratch-Off

Scratch art, or sgraffito, can create bold decoration or subtle accent. Create a hidden rainbow. Then reveal your design one scratch at a time. Scratching off that last layer can be fun and rewarding!

1 Create an abstract pattern using oil pastels. Use a heavyweight paper and press hard.

2 For the best effect, continue layering until you have a thick base of oil pastel.

3 Cover your drawing with a thick layer of black oil pastel. The black layer should almost cover the base layer completely.

4 Choose a tool for scratching. Some good scratching tools include:
   - teeth from a comb
   - clay loops
   - toothpicks
   - pens with the ink removed
   - steel wool
   - paintbrush handle

5 Scratch your design into the black oil pastel.

Scratchboard, gessoed board, or heavyweight pastel paper are best for this project.

3

For greatest effect, let your colored layer set overnight before adding the black layer.

Use a vacuum to pick up the bits of scratched-off pastel as you go.

4

5

Batik Heat

Get inspired by batik! Batik is a fabric dying technique from Indonesia. Hot wax is applied to cloth. Then the fabric is dyed. The wax is removed, leaving behind a pattern or design. White glue and soft pastels are safer and easier than wax and dye. Shine some light on this sensational style with a soft sun.

continued on next page

To give this project a twist, replace the glue with oil pastels. Use watercolors instead of soft pastels.

1 Lightly sketch your design onto your paper. Use a pastel or colored pencil in a similar color to your paper so the lines won't show later.

2 Trace your design with white glue. Start from the inside and work your way toward the paper's edges.

3 When you are happy with your glue design, let it dry overnight.

5

4 Add color using soft pastels. Start coloring the center and work your way out. This will prevent smearing.

5 Paint the corners and use a makeup sponge to blend inward. Paint inside swirls, but let the blending color the outside.

Resist Painting

Batik is a form of resist painting. The glue resists paint and pigment, allowing the plain paper to show through. Tape, crayons and wax, masking fluid, and glue all work well for resist painting.

Soft Edges

Take advantage of the butcher paper's natural colors tone and test out bold, fantastic colors. A sweeping piece of art with no hard lines or edges will let this fantasy horse gallop across the page.

1 Tape the edges of your paper to keep it flat.

2 Loosely sketch the form of the horse. Try to feel the horse's breath, movement, and life in your sketch.

3 Begin adding highlights and reflections on the horse's body. Soft pastels work well for this.

4 Draw the horse's features in more detail. Use pastel pencils to add more definition. Follow and build on the highlights you drew in the previous step.

5 Add more color to the horse, giving it more dimension and shape.

6 Add the horse's mane and muscles.

7 Finish with white highlights to give your horse a sunkissed look.

8 Drag pastels flat across the paper for a scumbling effect.

Butcher paper is good for more than sketching. It can also be used to protect your work surface. Tape a piece of butcher paper down to keep your table paint and pigment free.

Displaying Your Art

Although time does not cause pastels to fade, light will. Protect your finished pastel art by matting and framing it. Both matting and glass protect your art from dust and dirt, and prevent smudging.

Fixatives help "set" the pastels. They ensure the pastels cannot be brushed off. Fixatives can be hazardous, however. Wear a mask while spraying, and use only in a well-ventilated area. Be careful not to overuse fixative. Too much can dissolve pigment and change your painting's colors.

Butcher paper can be found at restaurant, teaching, and art supply stores.

Color Matching

Challenge yourself and take cookies and milk to the next level of sweetness. Use your artistic eye to pick out the base colors in a photograph. Then stick to them! Using only a few hues can be more freeing than having to choose from an entire rainbow. If sweets aren't your thing, don't get discouraged—any photo will do.

If you have a hard time matching colors, look online. There are many free tools that will help you pull colors directly from your photo. A visit to a paint store might help too. Check out the wall of paint swatches to find the right shades of color.

1 Select a photograph. Try to find a photo that has only four or five colors throughout.

2 Tape your paper down. Mask off an area of a similar shape and size to your photograph.

3 Use a gray pastel to start your sketch. Look carefully at shape and scale. Try to keep your sketch as close to the photograph as possible.

4 Begin filling in the basic shapes of the donut and straw, working toward matching the original photograph's color.

5 Blend the tan and brown pastels to give the milk a rich, creamy appearance.

6 Continue adding layers of color and shading. Give the donut more details, including a shiny glaze and scattering of sprinkles.

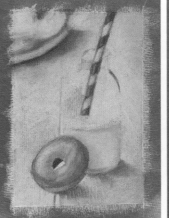

The gray underlayer is called grisaille. This layer establishes the painting's light and dark tones. It also gives the finished painting depth and dimension.

Pop Warhol

Celebrate pop culture with Pop Art. Color familiar objects with bright hues. Get inspired by movie stars, comic book characters, logos, and magazine ads.

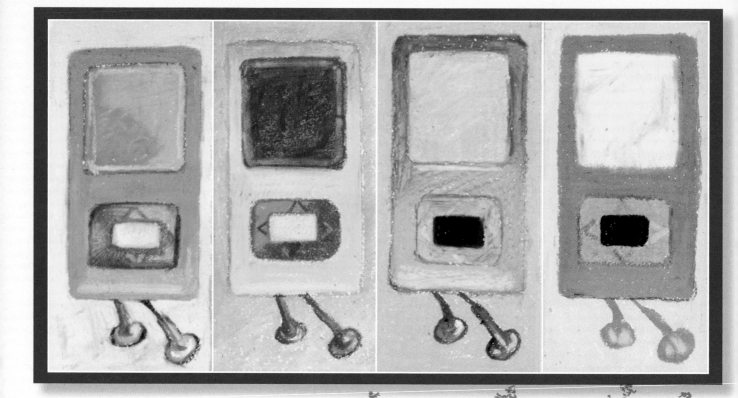

Andy Warhol

Andy Warhol (1928–1987) was an American artist active during the Pop Art movement (1950s–1960s). He is probably most famous for his silkscreen printing technique. This technique made it easy to mass produce art. His screenprints of Marilyn Monroe, Elvis Presley, Jackie Onassis, and soup cans are now famous icons.

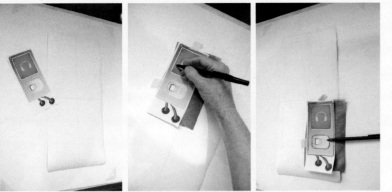

1 Divide a piece of pastel paper into four sections.

2 Print out a picture of your MP3 player, or sketch it onto a piece of paper.

3 Place your MP3 player on top of a piece of transfer paper. Place both papers onto a section of your pastel paper. Use a pen or mechanical pencil to trace the MP3 player onto your pastel paper.

4 Repeat step 3 until each section of your paper has an MP3 player in it.

Transfer paper is a special kind of paper coated with a layer of graphite. Tracing over the graphite transfers the image to the pastel paper.

5 Color each section with oil pastels. Try different color combinations for each section. Use bright colors with high contrasts.

For help choosing colors, do an Internet search for "pop art color palettes." Many Warhol-inspired palettes are available for comparison.

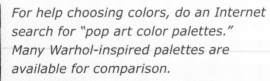

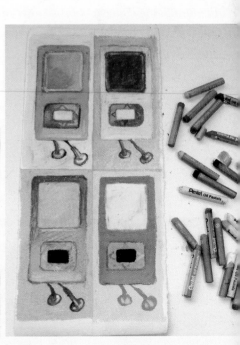

Street Sense

Never feel limited to flat pages in a studio! Get outside and explore the world of 3D chalk art. Artists around the world are taking to the street and bringing realistic drawings to life.

Get the OK before you start! Check with business owners, parks and recreation departments, or homeowners before sketching on the sidewalk.

Full-time chalk artists use professional-quality soft pastels. You will go through a lot of pastels this way. Chalk pastels are a cheaper choice for the beginner. Start there, and work your way up as your art improves.

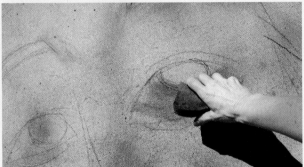

Use a grid to keep your layout to scale. Remember that your drawing will be longer than normal. The farthest-away points will be wider too.

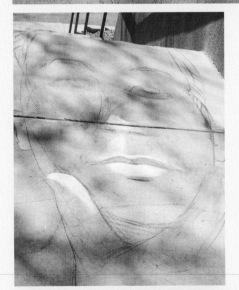

1 Choose a location where you can play with perspective. Try to pick a place that's out of the way and has little traffic.

2 Take a photo of the location from where your viewer will stand.

3 Sketch your photograph onto a piece of paper. Use this as your layout as you decide what to draw.

4 Use charcoal to sketch your layout onto the sidewalk. Keep a bucket of water and a sponge nearby to fix any mistakes.

5 Choose cool colors to fill in shadows, and warm colors as highlights. Try to use contrasting colors. Make sure you have enough of every color to fill in the entire area.

continued on next page

Image editing software can be a great tool. Some can show you how to draw your image to add perspective and dimension. There are also special grids online. Search for "3D anamorphic image grid."

6 Add shadows with blue pastels. Work light to dark, blending colors together. Try to start in the center and work your way toward the edges.

7 Continue building color and shading with yellows, oranges, and greens.

8 Color the area around the face and add final highlights. Then photograph your finished work!

Step away from your drawing often. This will ensure that the drawing stays balanced and to scale.

Tips For Success

- Use an old pillow or knee pads. These will save wear and tear on your knees and clothes.

- Wear old clothes! You'll be covered in pastel dust.

- Rags, plastic foam, and bits of carpet are great blending tools.

- Plan to paint all day. This is a big piece of artwork and will take a while to finish.

- Take photographs of your finished work! It might not be there tomorrow.

- Some chalk artists "prime" the sidewalk with a thin layer of tempera paint. The paint helps the chalk stick, and washes away with rain.

- If the weather turns against you, try covering your art with plastic sheeting and duct tape. It may help save your masterpiece.

Kurt Wenner

American Kurt Wenner invented 3D pavement art in 1984. In 1982 he quit his job as a NASA illustrator to study Renaissance art. He saw that Renaissance painters used perspective to create optical illusions. Wenner borrowed that idea. When viewed from the wrong angle, Wenner's paintings look strange. But when seen from the right spot, they pop or sink from the ground.

Overlapping layers of pastels can create a piece of art that's rich and full of color. Each type of pastel brings its own touch to this softly shaded sunset.

Use paper heavy enough to stand up to multiple layers. Sanded pastel paper or other heavily textured papers will work best.

1 Use a combination of hard and soft pastels to create a vivid blue sky. Blend with water or a makeup sponge to swirl your sky's colors together.

2 Choose a contrasting color for the ground. Apply using similar techniques from step 1.

3 Once the background looks the way you want, set the pastels with a light layer of fixative, if desired.

4 Add a layer of trees using oil pastels. Scumbling produces a nice, layered texture over the hard and soft pastels.

5 Use light layers of pastel pencils to create shades of light and color.

6 Use white oil pastels on areas you want to stand out.

7 Continue layering oil pastels and pastel pencils until your painting feels complete.

Don't press too hard while layering pastels. A nice, light stroke will be just as effective.

Oil Paints

IN YOUR ART BOX

Load your brush and get familiar with
the most classic of paints. Oil paints
were first used in the 1300s. They
became widely used in Europe in
the 1500s. Artists liked that the
paint could be thickly applied
or used to add tiny detail.
They also can stand the
test of time.

OIL PAINTS

Oil paints are made with dry pigments
blended with an oil, usually linseed oil.
Because it takes the oil so long to dry, oil
paint is ideal for long projects.

Oil paints can also be blended to create realistic
color combinations. The slow drying time allows the
artist to create natural blends with many layers.

SURFACES

Because oil paints stay wet so long, they can rot or corrode painted surfaces. Canvases must be sealed to prevent the canvas from absorbing the oil. Untreated canvas will also cause your oil paints to appear dull. Canvas can be bought treated and untreated.

Wood panels, masonite boards, and pads of canvas paper can also be used.

BRUSHES AND KNIVES

Natural hair brushes are best for oil painting. They hold up well to oil paints and retain their shape. Brushes are usually made from the fur from members of the weasel family. Minks, kolinskies, and ermine are common. Squirrel, ox, goat, and skunk hair brushes are also used.

Brushes used for oil painting need to be cleaned after each use. Solvents such as turpentine or mineral spirits are traditionally used. Although they can be dangerous, some artists feel they are best at removing paint from brush bristles. Walnut or linseed oil, baby oil, or special brush soaps are safer, solvent-free choices. Wash brushes with mild soap and water before putting them away.

Knives and spatulas are helpful tools for any painter. Painting knives are used to apply paint. Palette knives are used to scrape paint and clean palettes. Spatulas can be used to mix paint and apply paint to the canvas.

Painting knives should be made of steel. The blades should not be too sharp. Sharp edges can cut into paint, canvas—and you. Edges can be dulled with sandpaper before use.

Steel painting knives shouldn't rust when used with oil paint.

TIPS AND TECHNIQUES

~Keep your palette organized. Try to place every color on the same spot on your palette each time. Eventually you'll remember where red is, instead of having to look every time.

~Oil crayons or pastels are other forms of oil paint. They are soft, pigmented sticks of wax and oil. Like oil paints, they can be built up in layers. They can also be thinned with mineral spirits and brushed on.

~Use the basic technique of fat over lean when using oil paints. Lean paint has been thinned or diluted. Fat paint has more oil. Lean paint dries faster. If you paint lean over fat, the paint may not stick. It may also dry unevenly, which causes cracks in your painting. So start with lean paint for your underpainting. Then build as you go.

~To keep your hands clean, wear latex gloves while painting and during cleanup. You can also use special barrier cream or shea butter. These will help protect you from toxic pigments.

~For further protection, thin paints with walnut or linseed oil, rather than turpentine. If you do use turpentine, be sure to dispose of it properly. Seal it well and take it to your local recycling center.

~To save paint for future uses, cover your palette tightly with plastic wrap. Then put it in the freezer. Discard any paint that has developed a "skin."

paint applied with palette knife; thinned paint applied with toothbrush

oil pastels

thickly-applied paint

layered paint

blended colors

circular brush strokes

wet brush onto dry paper

SEALING AND TONING

Applying gesso is an important step when using untreated canvas. Gesso is an acrylic sealer. It prevents oil from sinking into the canvas. It also gives the paint something to grab onto. Apply gesso to the canvas with a brush. Let it dry. Repeat steps to add a second and third layer.

Toning canvas is not always necessary. However, it gives your painting a base. It also helps the dark and light colors show up better.

First choose the color to tone your canvas. The toning paint should be a contrasting color to your finished project. Apply with a paintbrush or a piece of cheesecloth.

COLOR PALETTE

Oil paints come in many premixed colors. However, most artists start with a base palette of between eight and 12 main colors. Below is a list containing some of the more common colors:

Flake White, Cadmium Yellow, Cadmium Red, Permanent Rose, Permanent Alizarin Crimson, French Ultramarine, Cobalt Blue, Ultramarine, Prussian Blue, Raw Umber, Yellow Ochre, Burnt Sienna, Titanium White, Lamp Black

Some pigments are toxic. If you're not sure whether a pigment is toxic, check the label. Many toxic pigments have a metal in their name. Look for paints with barium, cadmium, cobalt, zinc, lead, chrome, and manganese.

Transparent and Opaque

Paint comes in transparent and opaque. Transparent paint allows light through. Opaque paint does not. Start your painting with opaque paint. Then add details and shadows with transparent layers.

Compare how transparent and opaque paints behave when applied in layers. The base layer disappears under the opaque paint. The base is always visible under the transparent paint.

opaque

transparent

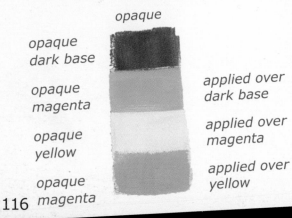

opaque dark base

opaque magenta

opaque yellow

opaque magenta

applied over dark base

applied over magenta

applied over yellow

transparent dark base

transparent magenta

transparent yellow

transparent magenta

1 Sketch out your solar system. Use a compass to draw planets.

2 Mix a transparent blue for the sky. Paint the background and around the circles. Don't worry about being perfect—the planets will be painted with opaque paint, so any mistakes will be covered. Let dry completely.

3 To add stars, grab an old toothbrush. Thin white paint with gel medium. Dip the toothbrush bristles into the paint. Gently tap the head of the toothbrush over your painting. This will spatter white stars across the sky.

4 Paint the planets with a variety of opaque paints. Let this layer dry completely.

5 Add land and oceans to your planets with transparent paint. Experiment by layering many different colors over the base coat.

Which Is It?

Many paint makers mark their tubes as opaque or transparent. Check your tube for small circles. A filled-in circle means the paint is opaque. An open circle means the paint is transparent.

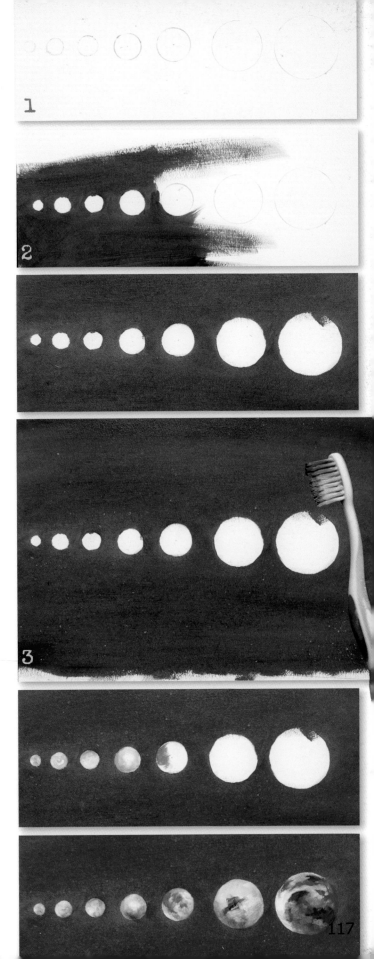

Tiny Art

Drawing thumbnails helps you plan ahead. You can decide what part of the painting will be the central focus. They also help you figure out the light and dark shades of the painting, called values.

Once you have a thumbnail sketch, you can turn it into a miniature painting. Painting in miniature allows you to work out any problem areas before starting your full-sized masterpiece.

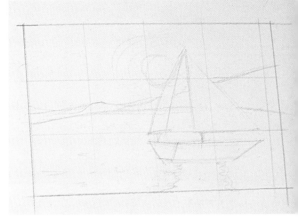

1 Sketch your rough design onto tracing paper. Draw in light and shaded areas.

2 Draw a grid on the tracing paper and over the rough design.

3 Draw a grid onto another piece of paper. Use this paper for your miniature painting.

4 Copy the tracing paper grid square by square onto the new grid. Keep this drawing clean; do not add light and shadows. You will paint those in later.

5 Once your miniature sketch is complete, prepare your palette. Mix darks and lights of contrasting hues.

6 Identify your darkest and lightest areas first. Block these areas with paint. Pay more attention to the tones and contrast, rather than detail work.

7 Add the medium blocks of color to bring your miniature painting together.

8 Add any details you may have missed.

continued on next page

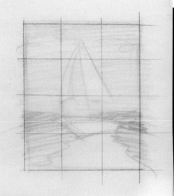

Another Angle

If your first thumbnail didn't turn out the way you wanted, try another! There are many ways to approach art. Switch up the painting's focus, tones, and values. This variation has a layer of light opaque paint added first. This layer will show through as you paint over it. Small changes can create a completely different piece of art.

1 Create a sketch and transfer it using the grid technique.

2 Lay a base layer of light opaque paint anywhere you want to represent natural light.

3 Add increasingly dark colors over the base layer. This will build contrast with your color values.

Impasto Owl

Impasto painting is the thick application of paint directly onto the canvas. Paintings with this technique can have an almost three-dimensional look.

continued on next page

1 Pencil the shape of the owl onto the canvas.

2 Use a brush to roughly paint the background. Flat bristled brushes work best for this.

The Starry Night

The Starry Night is one of the most well-known impasto paintings. It was done by Dutch artist Vincent Van Gogh (1853–1890). He painted it in 1889. He finished it in just three days. See also Impressionism (1874–1886) and Expressionism (early 1900s–1925).

3 Use a palette knife to outline the owl's facial feathers. Squeeze paint directly from the tube and onto the palette knife.

4 Overlap with inner layers. Continue overlapping to build texture. Clean your palette knife in between colors.

5 Work from the middle of the painting toward the edges.

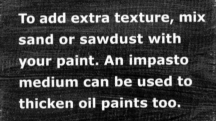

Paint applied too thickly may crack as it dries, so take care not to add too many layers.

To add extra texture, mix sand or sawdust with your paint. An impasto medium can be used to thicken oil paints too.

Indirect Sushi

Indirect painting is the traditional technique used with oil paints. Artists begin with an underpainting called grisaille, or gray painting. Underpainting establishes a painting's dark and light tones. Then regular paint is applied with glazes and scumbles. Because indirect painting requires underlayers to be dry, it is not for the impatient!

Glazes and Scumbles

A **glaze** is a transparent layer of dark paint over light opaque paint. The opaque paint must be completely dry before applying the transparent layer. The transparent paint must be thinned. Glazes give paintings an appearance of depth.

A **scumble** is a layer of light paint applied over darker paint. Like glazing, the dark paint should be completely dry. However, it is not thinned. Scumbling is a great way to add light to your painting.

1 Lightly sketch your drawing onto paper. Choose colored paper that's not too light or too dark. This will make it easier to build the painting's values (light and dark parts) as you go.

2 Start with the grisaille layer. Mix black and white or Burnt Umber and white. See how many different grays you can create with those two colors.

3 Begin by painting the darkest areas. Work your way to the lightest spots.

4 Add highlights in white and light gray. Let the underpainting dry completely. This will take two or three days.

5 Build your middle layer by scumbling opaque paint. Let the middle layer dry completely before continuing.

6 Add final glaze layers with thinned transparent paints. These layers will change the colors of the scumbled opaque paints.

Use the paper's texture to bring out the textures of your painting.

Direct Sushi

Apply the first layers with a large brush or rag. This will keep your base layer simple.

Direct painting, also called alla prima, is a bright, fresh take on oil painting. Alla prima paintings are completed in a single session.

Plan your color placement in advance. Since you'll be painting in a single session, your underlayers won't have a chance to dry. When working with wet paint, using dark colors over light will cause your paint layers to blend and appear muddy. Color the dark areas first. Then use brighter paint to mimic natural light.

1 Mix all the colors you may need onto your palette before beginning.

2 Lightly sketch your sushi. Plan which colors will go where.

3 Apply the middle tones to the canvas. Lay down basic shapes. Clean your brush between strokes and different applications of color.

4 Add highlights of color. Vary your brush strokes to represent your subject's texture. Objects in the background will have less color contrast. Objects in the foreground will need to pop.

5 Paint foreground objects with high-contrast colors and shorter strokes.

What's the Difference?

Compare the two sushi paintings. You'll notice that the direct sushi looks brighter but flatter.

Indirect painting uses layers of transparent paint over opaque. The canvas, the opaque layer, and the transparent layer can be seen in different parts of the painting. This allows light and color to interact with each other, creating depth.

Direct painting uses only opaque paint. Light bounces right off the surface of the painting. This creates a bright, reflective picture.

Seurat Dots

Far away, you see a painting with vivid color and dazzling light. Up close, you see small dots and tiny brush strokes. Each dot is a single color. The dots have come together to create an entire picture! This technique is called pointillism. French painter Georges Seurat (1859–1891) was the inventor of this technique. His most famous painting, *A Sunday on La Grande Jatte*, was created with pointillism. Borrow his technique to create this dazzling, dotted dragonfly.

Neo-What?

Georges Seurat led the Neo-Impressionistic movement (1886–1891). Painting techniques of this movement were more scientific. They explored combining separate, overlapping colors, rather than colors traditionally blended together.

1. Prime your wood panel with linseed oil. Linseed oil will preserve the wood. It acts as a barrier between the wood and the paint. Without this barrier, the paint's oil will rot the wood.

2. Sketch a rough layout of your design in pencil.

3. Mix your color palette.

4. Use round brushes or cotton swabs to create dots on your wood panel. Begin with the green background.

5. Once the background is complete, fill in the butterfly.

Think about which color blends look best together. Use similar colors to create shading. Use complementary colors to help your butterfly stand out.

Picasso's Pets

Spanish painter Pablo Picasso (1881–1973) was well known for his Blue and Rose Periods. Try copying his style by sticking with only reds and blues. Then add highlights from the opposite color palette.

Blue

1 Choose a pet whose mood matches the blue palette.

2 Use parchment paper to encourage soft brush strokes. Use painter's tape to flatten the paper and create neat edges.

3 Sketch your layout onto the paper.

4 Block the middle tones of color. Start with the largest areas. Work your way toward the smaller spaces.

5 Mix your red palette. Try for reds with a cooler tone. Use this palette to add fur texture and color.

6 Switch back to blue. Add detail to the pet's eyes and nose.

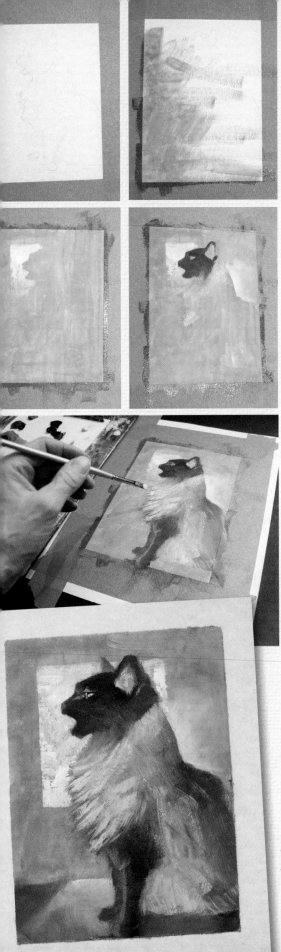

Rose

For the rose painting, start with a transparent background. Tone the entire background with a single warm color. Then find your subject by building layers of color.

1. Copy steps 1–3 from the Blue project, but pick a pet whose mood matches the rose palette.

2. Cover the paper with an underlayer of transparent Burnt Orange. Leave a small square unpainted.

3. Create the subject's form over the top of your underlayer. Build the painting with multiple layers of color from your palette.

4. Paint in fur texture and color.

5. Add detail to the pet's eyes and nose.

6. Paint color highlights to the unpainted square. Use colors from the blue palette.

Blue and Rose

Picasso's Blue Period paintings were done in shades of blue. The subjects he painted were sad and gloomy. During his Rose Period, Picasso's color choices became brighter and warmer. He often painted with pinks and reds.

Limit your palette to a basic red/blue, a secondary red/blue (such as orange/turquoise), black, and white.

131

Plein Air

Why stay cooped up inside when there's plenty to paint outdoors? Gather your supplies and make your way outside! *Plein air* means "in the open air" in French. Create a portrait of your favorite person while getting some fresh air together.

1. Choose a location that will provide good light for at least an hour. Be sure your subject will be comfortable and relaxed sitting there the entire time.

2. Prepare your supplies before your subject arrives.

3. Sketch your subject in charcoal. Pay particular attention to the area around your subject, known as negative space.

4. Add shading to create a greater sense of the subject's form.

5. Working quickly, block in color and tone. A large brush will work best. Take a photograph of your subject in case you need to add more detail later.

6. Begin adding the model's base skin tone. Add base layers for the model's hair and clothing too.

Modern Technology

Plein air painting became popular in the late 1800s. Before, artists had to mix their own paint. This was time consuming. But in 1867 the first premixed paint was sold. Premixed oil paints in tubes were released soon after. Around the same time, portable easels were invented. These inventions made it easy for artists to paint anywhere they wanted.

French Impressionist artists fully embraced the plein air movement. See Claude Monet and Pierre-Auguste Renoir.

continued on next page

7 Continue adding to background tones.

8 Add lights/darks and warm/cool tones to the skin and hair. Pay close attention to the natural skin tones of your model and how the light affects them.

9 Continue building layers of color. Add details of the model's eyes and lips. Try to complete work on your model before the light changes. You can always finish the background later.

Aim to start painting in the late afternoon. The sunlight will be at its brightest.

Tips for Successful Plein Air Painting

Scout locations the day before you begin painting. Observe the location around the same time of day that you plan to paint.

When you find the perfect location, make sure it's out of the way. If it's near a home or business, get permission to paint there.

Take pictures while you paint. This will let you go back and check shadows and sunlight later.

Pack light! If you don't need an easel, don't bring it. A board to tape your canvas to works just as well and weighs a lot less. Keep your palette small, and your brush choices even smaller.

Don't skimp on water! Bring plenty, both for your brushes and for yourself and your model.

A roll of paper towels is essential. Weigh the roll down with a PVC pipe small enough to fit inside the center tube. You can also store your brushes inside the pipe.

Be courteous! Clean up after yourself, and thank anyone who may have given you permission to paint.

Not ready for a human subject? Try painting a landscape or cityscape instead.

In the Style Of

Reinvent the salad bar with this fresh and fruity painting! Play with your food and explore the works of Italian painter Giuseppe Arcimboldo. How many features can you create to make edible art?

1 Before you begin, think about the shapes of your subject. Keep in mind the colors and textures of each piece of food. Examine the foods and how the light hits each piece. Play with the arrangement until it looks exactly how you want.

2 Prime a piece of masonite board with linseed oil.

Be sure to use hard-pressed masonite board for your painting. Other kinds are too absorbent and fall apart. Both sides of the board can be painted on.

continued on next page

About Arcimboldo

Giuseppe Arcimboldo (1527–1593) is best known for his heads made out of food. He took everyday objects, such as fruit, vegetables, and roots, and arranged them to look like his portrait subject. See *Vegetables in a Bowl* or *The Gardener, The Lady of Good Taste*, and *The Four Seasons in One Head*.

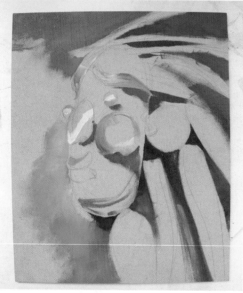

For something different, try fluorescent or other bright colors, or use different objects to create your face. How about cookie eyes and a snack cake smile?

3 Lightly sketch your composition onto the board.

4 Paint the dark background colors.

5 Paint the background shapes and colors of the fruits and vegetables.

Funny Foods

Arcimboldo began painting food around the time Christopher Columbus reached America. Food never before seen, such as corn and eggplant, were sent to Europe. Artists were hired to visually record these new finds. Follow Arcimboldo's lead and paint foods unfamiliar to you.